NATIONAL
GEOGRAPHIC

On Safari

Gare Thompson

Contents

The Serengeti

Let's go on a safari. The word *safari* comes from an Arabic word that means "journey." A hundred years ago, people went on a safari to hunt wild animals. Today, people go on a safari to observe wild animals and take pictures of them.

Land and Climate

We are going to the Serengeti Plain in east Africa. The name Serengeti means "endless plains." The Serengeti are

the grasslands of Africa. Here you will see tall grasses and a few trees. You'll see small rivers, lakes, and even swamps.

On the Serengeti, the climate is usually warm and dry. There are two rainy seasons. The heaviest rain falls from March to May. Some rain falls from October to November. At other times it is dry.

The Animals of the Serengeti

Millions of large animals roam these grasslands. Many of them live in national parks. The government sets up these parks to protect Africa's rich wildlife. Here you will see many different animals. There are lions, cheetahs, zebras, and elephants. There are giraffes, monkeys, and lots of water animals. The Serengeti is the perfect place to study animals.

AFRICA

SERENGETI PLAIN

Many scientists come here to study animals. They watch how the animals act. They track them to see where they go. They see how they take care of their young.

On our safari, we'll study three very different animals. Stay together. Take careful notes. Draw pictures if you want to. Try not to scare the animals.

Giraffes

Let's Look at Giraffes

The giraffe is the tallest of all land animals. Its long neck is what makes it so tall. The giraffe has seven bones in its neck. The giraffe's bones are huge! Most male giraffes stand about 19 feet (6 meters) tall. Females are a little shorter.

Giraffes have dark brown spots. The spots form a pattern on their yellow fur. The spots are pretty to look at, but they also help protect giraffes. When giraffes are in the trees, their spots help to hide them.

Notice the giraffe's large head. The first thing you probably see are its horns. Some giraffes have two horns, but others have four.

Can you find its nostrils? They are the two slits at the end of its nose. A giraffe's nostrils can open and close. Winds blow sand and dirt around. The giraffe closes its nostrils to keep out sand and dirt.

Sight is the giraffe's most important sense. Look at its large eyes high on its head. It is the first animal on the Serengeti to spot an enemy. When a giraffe sees an enemy, it runs away. Giraffes have long legs. They can run fast. Sometimes, they use their hard hooves to kick an enemy. But giraffes are peaceful animals. They do not have many enemies.

Eating in the Wild

Watch a giraffe eat. It stretches its long neck to the top of a tree. There it finds fresh green leaves. We can see them eating from an acacia tree. Acacia leaves are their favorite food. But some giraffes also eat twigs and thorns. Eating from trees like this is called browsing.

Giraffes have very long tongues. They can be over a foot and a half (46 centimeters) long. Giraffes curl their long tongues around the leaves and tear them off. Most animals cannot reach food this high. A giraffe eats like a cow or sheep. It chews its cud. That means that it chews food two times before digesting it.

Giraffes can go a long time without drinking water. But when they do drink, they have to be careful. Look at how the giraffe drinks water. It must spread its legs far apart to be able to reach the water.

Giraffes usually go to a watering hole together. Otherwise, a lion might attack while they are drinking. Look at their position. See how easily a lion could attack them.

Giraffe Families

Giraffes live together in small groups. The young giraffes play together. Several of the female giraffes, called aunts, watch the young. The aunts take care of the young while the other giraffes feed. They clean them. They help them get food. They protect them.

Female giraffes can have babies when they are five years old. The baby, or calf, is born after 15 months. At birth, the calf is about 6 feet (2 meters) tall. The mother stands when giving birth. This means that the calf drops to the ground when it is born. But it is not hurt. Within 30 minutes, the calf can stand on its long, wobbly legs.

How do giraffes sleep? They can sleep standing up or lying down. But giraffes do not sleep for long periods of time. Let's time them. Most sleep for only three or four minutes. Then they wake up. They doze more than sleep. At dawn, they get up. It is time to start another day.

Cheetahs

Let's Look at Cheetahs

The cheetah looks like a big cat. It weighs from 80 to 140 pounds (34-74 kilograms). The cheetah is large but fast. It is the fastest land animal. The cheetah can run over 60 miles (97 kilometers) per hour. That is as fast as cars go!

The cheetah has a body that helps it run fast. It has long, thin legs. Its legs may be thin, but they are powerful. Its legs give it great speed.

The cheetah has a small head and a flat face. It has large eyes and excellent eyesight. It can see long distances.

See the cheetah's tan coat. It has black spots on it. With its spotted coat, the cheetah is hard to see in the tall grass. The cheetah also has spots on its tail. Look at the end of its tail. It looks like a paintbrush.

The cheetah has different paws than most cats. Can you guess how its paws are different? A cheetah cannot pull its claws all the way in and out like other cats. It has short claws that help the cheetah grip the ground as it runs. Its pads are hard like tire treads. This helps the cheetah make sharp turns. Few animals can escape a cheetah.

Eating in the Wild

Unlike the giraffe, the cheetah eats meat. It hunts its prey. The cheetah is a good hunter. Let's observe the cheetah hunting.

First, the cheetah uses its eyes to spot its prey. Most cheetahs hunt during the day when it is easy to see. Cheetahs hunt when it is cool. They hunt in the early morning or the late afternoon.

The cheetah follows, or stalks, its prey from a distance. It often follows herds of antelopes or gazelles. Look! There's a gazelle. The cheetah has waited for it to wander away from its herd. It may be an animal that is hurt or slow.

Now, the cheetah gives chase. It quickly brings down its prey. Its powerful jaws grip the gazelle. The animal cannot breathe and dies. The cheetah has its meal.

The cheetah rests before it eats. Sometimes, other animals try to steal its food while the cheetah rests. But these animals have to move fast or hope that the cheetah has fallen asleep. Animals know that they cannot outrun the cheetah.

Cheetah Families

Many cheetahs live alone. Others live in small groups. Listen to them. They do not roar like other large cats. They whine or growl. A cub makes a chirping sound to call its mother.

The female gives birth after carrying her babies for three months. She has a litter of four to six cubs. The cubs are small when they are born. The mother finds a quiet, hidden spot for the cubs. Look at this tall grass. This hidden spot will keep the cubs safe. Cubs are a favorite food for lions.

The cubs begin to follow the mother around when they are six weeks old. As they play, they learn to hunt. See the cubs pretending to hunt. Sometimes the cubs chase prey that is too big for them to kill. But they keep trying.

The cubs stay with their mother until they are about 18 months old. Then they leave. Often, the male cubs stay together. They form a group that can last for the rest of their lives.

Elephants

Let's Look at Elephants

What is the first thing that you observe about elephants? It probably is their size. Elephants are the biggest land animal in the world. Male elephants weigh about 6 tons (5,500 kilograms)! Do you see how thick their skin is? This helps protect them. They can go through thick thorns without being hurt. What else do you see?

Elephants have tusks. Look at how large the elephant's tusks are. Tusks are teeth that never stop growing. They are long, pointed, and curved. They are made out of ivory. Hunters kill elephants for their tusks.

See the elephant's trunk. An elephant uses its trunk for holding things, eating, and drinking. Elephants also use their trunks to spray themselves. This cools them off and gets rid of bugs, too. Watch out! A trunk filled with water can soak you!

The elephant is very large, but its eyes are small. They are about the size of a golf ball. What color are they? Most elephants' eyes are a golden or green color. Look at its long lashes. Its lashes help protect its eyes.

Elephants are smart animals. They have the biggest brain of all land animals. Let's watch them in the wild and see how smart they are!

Eating in the Wild

Remember how big elephants are? Well, they have to eat a lot of food. Most elephants eat about 300 pounds (136 kilograms) of food each day! That is why we see the elephants moving. They are always looking for food.

Elephants eat many things. They eat grass and leaves. They also eat bulbs, berries, and tree bark. Like the giraffe, elephants love to eat acacia trees. But the elephants do not eat the leaves at the top.

Watch them. See how the elephant gathers food with its trunk and puts it in its mouth. Elephants can also use their tusks to strip off bark from trees. They can use their trunks to pick up nuts from the ground.

It's easy to tell when elephants have been in an area. You can tell by looking at the bushes. Elephants use their trunks to dig bushes out of the ground. They are trying to get at the roots. Elephants feed on roots.

Elephant Families

Elephants live in family groups called herds. Elephants can live to be 60 or 70 years old. So, these herds stay together for a long time.

See those two elephants with their trunks together? They are "kissing." Elephants play and live together. The male elephant is called a bull. The female is called a cow.

Like the giraffe, the elephant gives birth standing up. But the elephant carries its baby almost two years before it is born. The young calf gets milk from its mother until it is about three years old. Then it starts to eat grass. The calves stay with the herd until they are about 13 years old. Then they often join another herd.

Unlike giraffes or cheetahs, elephants sniff danger. They use their trunk to do this. When an animal comes too near, elephants flap their ears and make a frightening sound. Then they charge at top speed. The elephants work as a group to protect each other.

Elephants may be big, but they are gentle and caring. They live together and look out for each other much the way our own families do.

What Did You Observe?

How are these animals alike and different? Think about their special features – how they look and what they can do. Think about what the animals eat, how they take care of their families, and how they live.